For my Lisa—A. B. H.

For Stéphanie, Benoit, and Romain—B. L.

2017 First US edition
Translation copyright © 2017 by Charlesbridge Publishing. Translated by Julie Cormier.
All rights reserved, including the right of reproduction in whole or in part in any form.
Charlesbridge and colophon are registered trademarks of Charlesbridge Publishing, Inc.

Published by Charlesbridge
85 Main Street
Watertown, MA 02472
(617) 926-0329
www.charlesbridge.com

First published in France in 2015 by Gallimard Jeunesse as *Nina*
by Alice Brière-Haquet and Bruno Liance.
Copyright © Gallimard Jeunesse, 2015 • www.gallimard-jeunesse.fr

Library of Congress Cataloging-in-Publication Data
Names: Brière-Haquet, Alice, 1979– I Liance, Bruno.
Title: Nina: jazz legend and civil-rights activist Nina Simone /
Alice Brière-Haquet ; illustrated by Bruno Liance.
Other titles: Nina: jazz legend and civil-rights activist Nina Simone. English
Description: First US edition. I Watertown, MA : Charlesbridge, 2017.
Identifiers: LCCN 2017000466 (print) I LCCN 2017000892 (ebook) I
ISBN 9781580898270 (reinforced for library use) I ISBN 9781632896919 (ebook) I
ISBN 9781632896926 (ebook pdf)
Subjects: LCSH: Simone, Nina, 1933–2003—Juvenile literature. I
Women singers—United States—Biography—Juvenile literature. I
Singers—United States—Biography—Juvenile literature.
Classification: LCC ML3930.S553 B713 2017 (print) I LCC ML3930.S553 (ebook) I
DDC 782.42164092 [B] —dc23
LC record available at https://lccn.loc.gov/2017000466

Printed in China
(hc) 10 9 8 7 6 5 4 3 2 1

Display type set in Barberry by Zakhar Yaschin
and Pinto No_1 by Georg Herold-Wildfellner
Text type set in ITC Kabel
Printed by 1010 Printing International Limited in Huizhou, Guangdong, China
Production supervision by Brian G. Walker
Designed by Sarah Richards Taylor

Nina

JAZZ LEGEND AND CIVIL-RIGHTS ACTIVIST NINA SIMONE

ALICE BRIÈRE-HAQUET

ILLUSTRATED BY BRUNO LIANCE

ini Charlesbridge

GO TO SLEEP, MY PRECIOUS ONE;
DAY IS DONE AND NIGHT IS NEAR.
WHEN YOU WAKE YOU'LL SEE THE SUN,
WISH YOU FOR A STAR TO STEER.

—LULLABY SUNG BY SINGER/SONGWRITER AND CIVIL-RIGHTS
ACTIVIST NINA SIMONE TO HER DAUGHTER

Dream, my baby, dream,
until you spread your wings. . . .

Hey my child, my sweet child . . . you are having
a hard time falling asleep tonight, so listen to my story.

It starts like stories often do, with a baby
wrapped in a white sheet and her mother
smiling at her.

This little baby was black.

This little baby was me.

I don't remember that, of course. My first childhood memory came a little bit later.

I must have been about three years old.

I thought the piano looked like there were fifty-two white teeth and thirty-six black teeth trapped in the keyboard. The black keys were smaller.

"The white keys are whole notes and the black
keys are flats, or half notes," my teacher explained.
I asked why.

"Because that's just the way it is."
Yes, that's the way it was. White was whole. Black was half. It was that way everywhere and for everyone.

I could have held it against people. Or worse, I
could've believed I was worth less than other people.

Black people were nothing but half notes on a huge ivory keyboard.

But no. I did not agree with this.

The notes had to mingle and dance together in the air so these lies would disappear.

Music has no color. In music there is only one rhythm. Only one heart.

Ba-boom.

Ba-boom.

One heartbeat per second, the same rhythm for everyone.

Standing on the bus with my eyes closed, I reminded myself of this.

The years went by. I played Mozart, Liszt, Beethoven, Chopin, Debussy.

I played all the important men in powdered wigs
from past centuries. I was talented. People told me so.

When I was twelve years old, our church asked
me to give a performance.

Mom sewed a beautiful white dress with pleats
and pretty ribbons.
God knows she was proud—her daughter was
giving a concert!

My mom, my sweet mom . . . She sat in the front row with her radiant smile.
Then white people arrived. She had to get up.

I squeezed my eyes tight so I could listen to my dreams dance in the air.

But there was nothing. Nothing except silence and injustice.

So I refused.

Right there, in front of black and white people. I didn't care. The only noise was my heart beating. And it was beating for my mother.

It was her right to be in the front row.

So Mom sat back down. She wasn't smiling anymore, and my fingers were trembling with anger.

But the concert was beautiful.

Hey child, my sweet child . . . Later, much later (in fact, you were already born!), a man arrived on our TV screens, on our radios, in our newspapers. And he said, "I have a dream."

Martin Luther King Jr. had a dream. He believed in it, and people followed him.

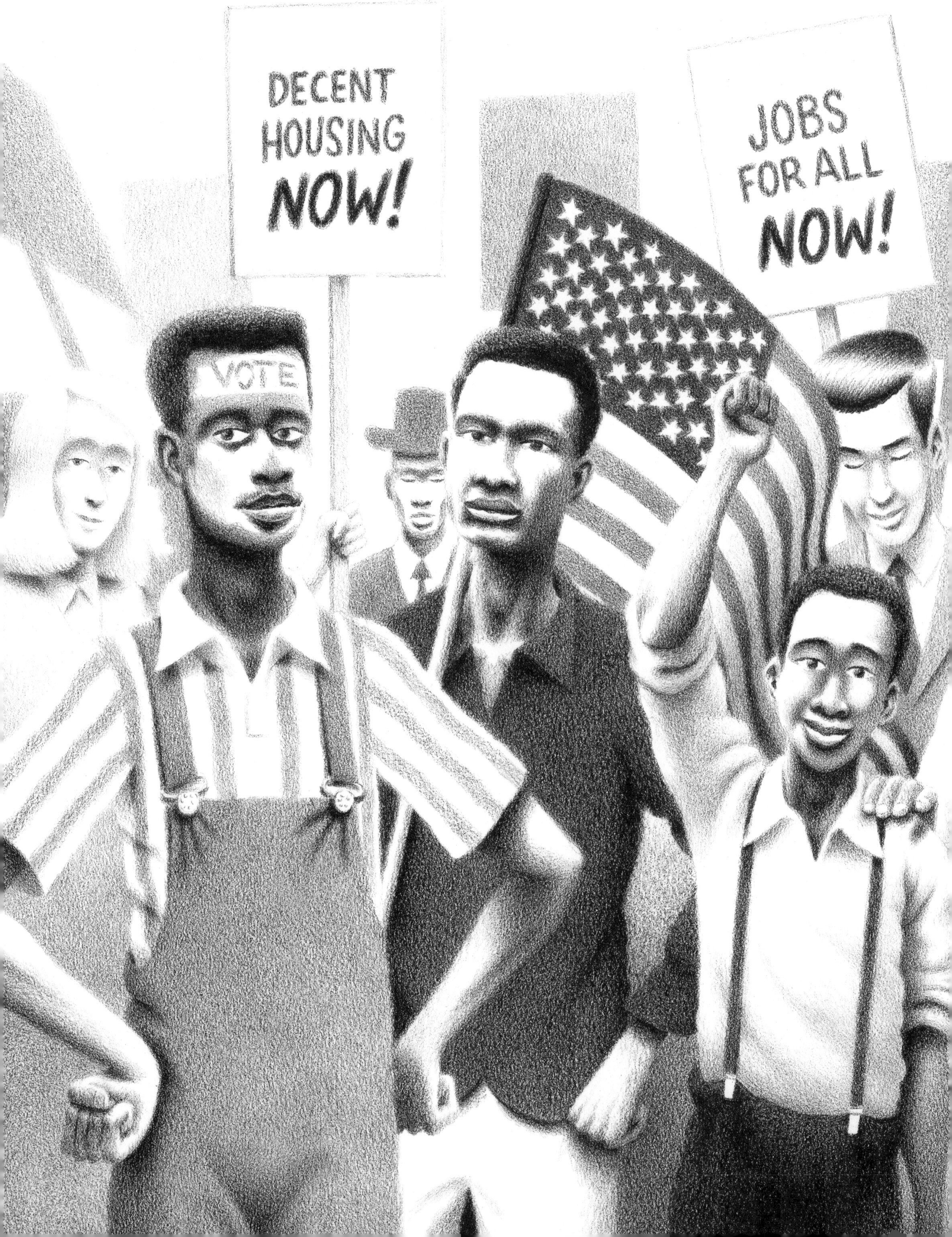
DECENT
HOUSING
NOW!
JOBS
FOR ALL
NOW!
VOTE

Martin's dream was my symphony. Black and white people could come together in the big dance of life.

Hey child, my sweet child . . . Sometimes it seems as if that dream came true! But the dream is fragile. You have to take care of it.

Dream, my baby, dream,

until you spread your wings. . . .